It's Raining Diamonds

(Small Book)

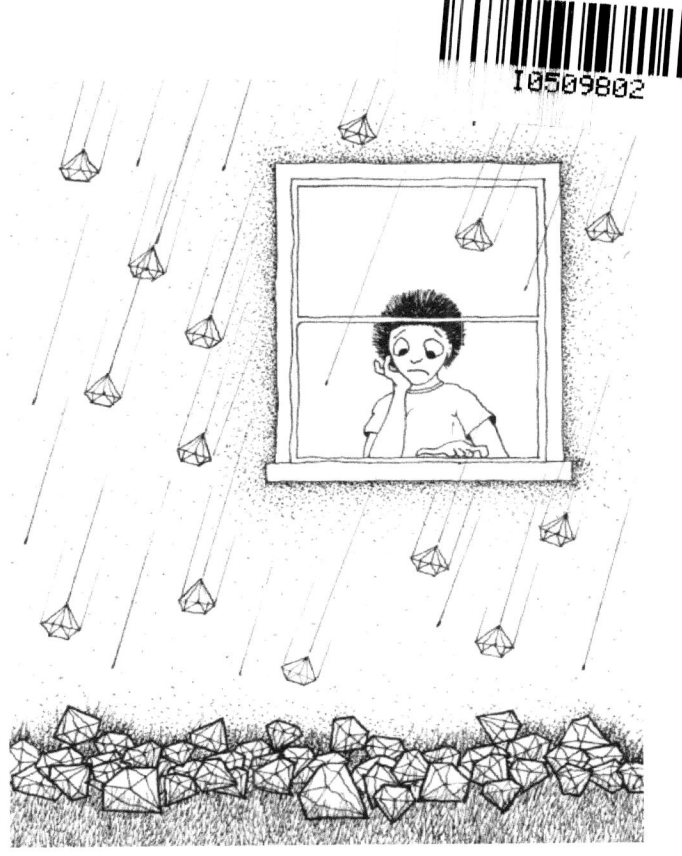

Peter Blueberry

*Thank you for the laughter
Olivia, Blake, Calvin, Dane, and
Rose.*

It's Raining Diamonds (Small Book)
© 2019 Peter Blueberry

All rights reserved. No part of this book may be reproduced in any manner whatsoever without the written permission of the author except in the case of brief quotations embedded in critical articles and reviews. Printed in the United States of America - Scary Black Goo Publishing. P.O.Box 188245, 1212 Broadway, Sacramento, CA 95818

Library of Congress Control Number: 2017951577

Table of Contents

4	In Between
6	Did The Sun Come Up
7	The Grumpy Old Man
8	Dragons Underneath
10	I Can't Go Out
11	Being Good Is Hard
12	My Pet Monster Fred
14	The Mountain Stream
16	It's Raining Diamonds
18	The Fly
19	Lying Up And . . .
	. . . Looking Down
21	Closet Pirates
22	Close To Shore
24	Baseball
25	Sun Up
26	I'm In Trouble Tomorrow
28	Have You Ever
30	Sitting In A Tree
31	It's Good To Know
32	*Questions*

In Between

Billy was filthy.
His clothes were disgustly,
And dirt was caked up his nose.

When he walked through the door
Muck covered the floor,
And behind him, a cloud of dust rose.

To the tub he was sent.
To get scrubbed, it was meant,
And, so, he took off his clothes.

But the only place clean
That could still be seen
Was in between **Billy's toes.**

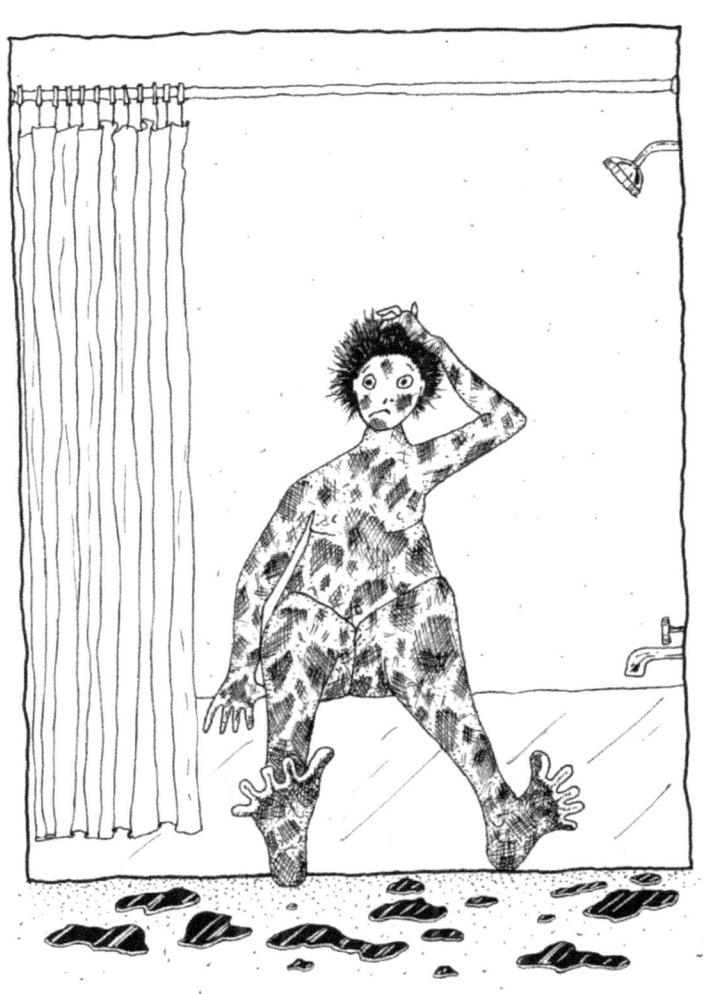

Did The Sun Come Up

I stayed in bed,
And covered my head.
The day I did not want to see.

It was one of those days
When it just doesn't pay
To crawl out from under the sheets.

So, I laid in the dark,
And I didn't embark
Outside and into the day.

But, I'd like to know, *Well, did it?*
And tell me if it's so.
Did the sun come up anyway?

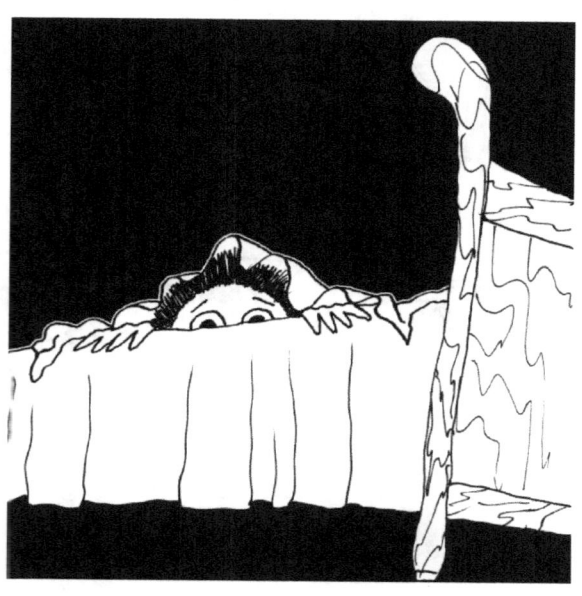

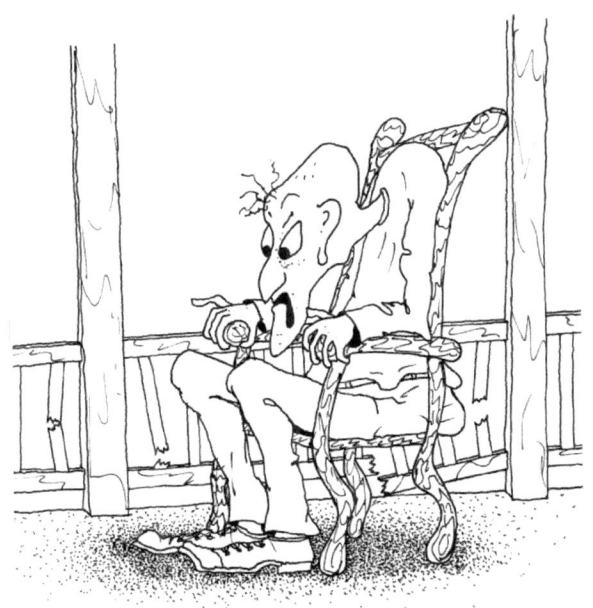

This seat's too grumpy!

The Grumpy Old Man

There's a grumpy old man.
In a grumpy old chair.
On a grumpy old porch.
With a grumpy old stare.

He's grumpy in the morning,
And he's grumpy at night.
He's grumpy when he's wrong,
And he's grumpy when he's right.

But, he wouldn't be so grumpy,
And I think what I say is fair.
If he'd just get off his grumpy old fanny,
And change his **grumpy old underwear.**

Dragons Underneath

There are cracks in the asphalt
That weren't there before.
People better be careful,
Or someone could get sore.

    Now, if you listen real closely,
    And put your ear to the ground.
    You can hear something moving.
    Like things bumping around.

My Dad says the cracks
Are from the sun's terrible heat.
But, I know why the asphalt's cracked;
There are dragons underneath.

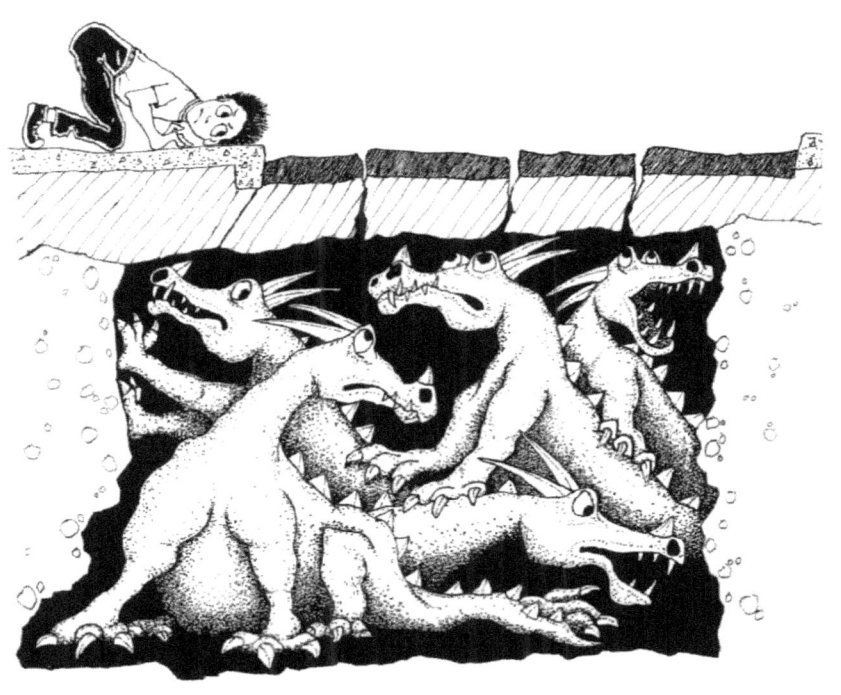

Shhh! I think I hear somebody listening.

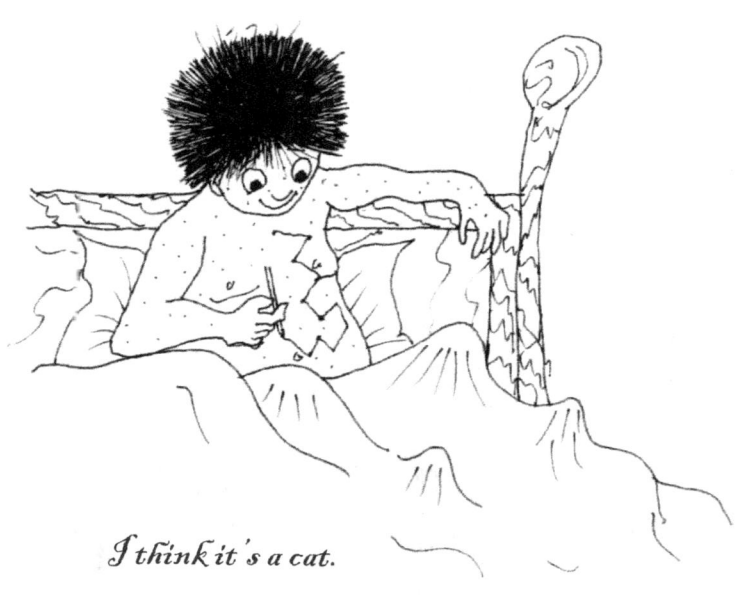

I think it's a cat.

I Can't Go Out

I can't go out and play today.
I'm covered in funny red spots.
My Mom says it's the Chicken Pox.
I'm just going to play **connect the dots.**

Being Good Is Hard

I'm trying to do what's right;
Be nice to my brother and sister.
Pick up all my toys,
And try not to bother or pester.

Be polite to people,
And do things in a proper way.
But being good is hard.
I know, **I tried it yesterday.**

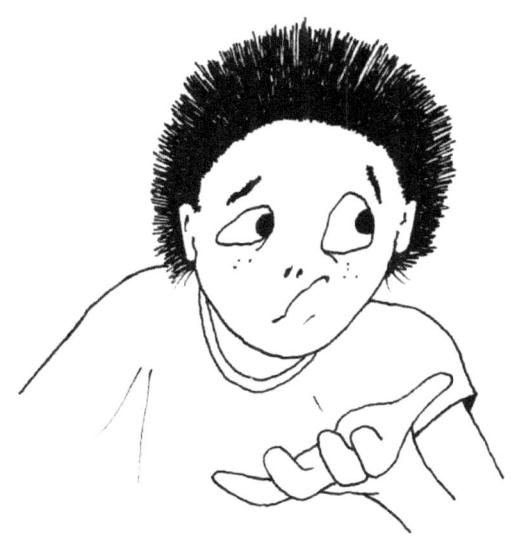

Ya want I should try it again?

My Pet Monster Fred

I have a pet monster
Who I've named Fred.
He's made from spare monster parts
From his toes up to his head.

> I found him in a garage sale.
> I paid a whole buck 35.
> He was stuffed in an old basket,
> And just barely alive.

I brought him home to my bedroom.
Washed off all the goop.
I put him in my bed for a week,
And fed him monster soup.

> Now he sits guarding my room
> In a nest at the foot of my bed.
> He scares all the other monsters away.
> **He's my pet monster Fred.**

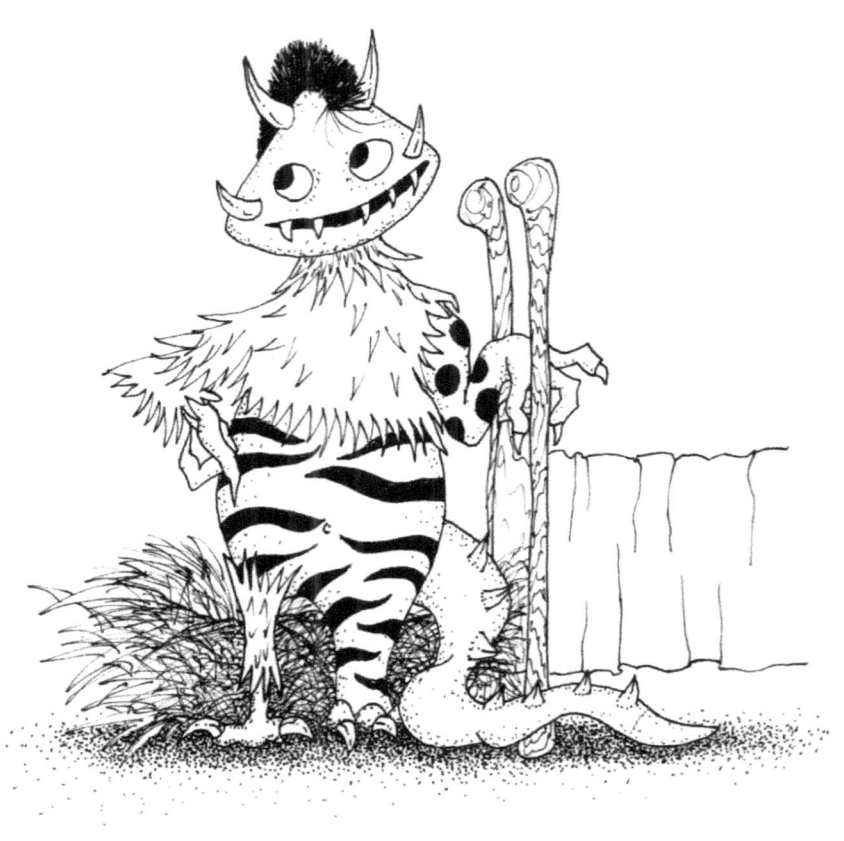

I just love my new nest.

The Mountain Stream

There is a mountain stream
That runs through the trees.
Winding like a slithering snake,
Dampening all the leaves.

Its cool air is so fresh.
Its water is so clean.
It's a beautiful thing to see
This precious mountain stream.

And if you ever go there,
And for a while you stay.
Pretend no one's ever been there,
And **give it back that way.**

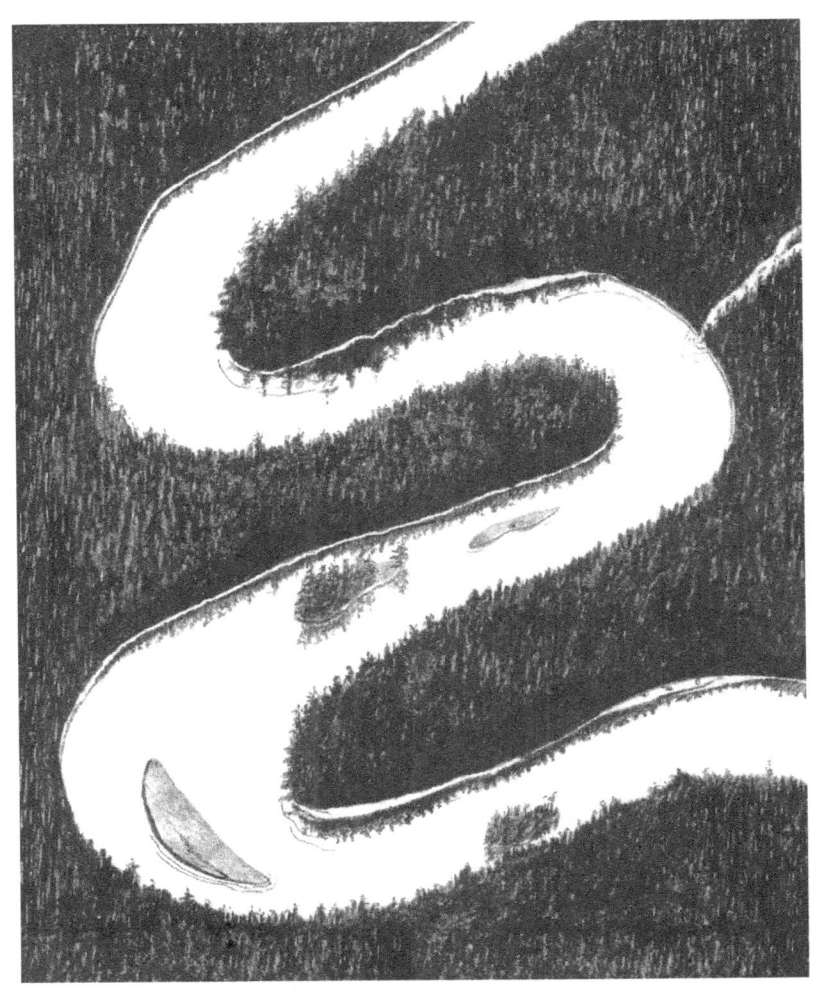

It's Raining Diamonds

It's raining diamonds,
    And I can't go out outside.
It's really raining diamonds.
    They're just falling from the sky.

I can see them everywhere.
    They're covering up the lawn.
But by the time I get to go outside
    The diamonds will be all gone.

Now all I can do is watch,
    And feel like a boy in a bubble.
I have to stay inside all day.
    Because I got into trouble.

You see, I didn't pick up my toys,
    And I didn't put my clothes away.
I tracked mud into the house,
    And I didn't do my chores today.

So, I'll just sit here and stare,
    And wallow in my sorrow.
I just hope the weather holds,
    And it rains **diamonds ...**
        ... again tomorrow.

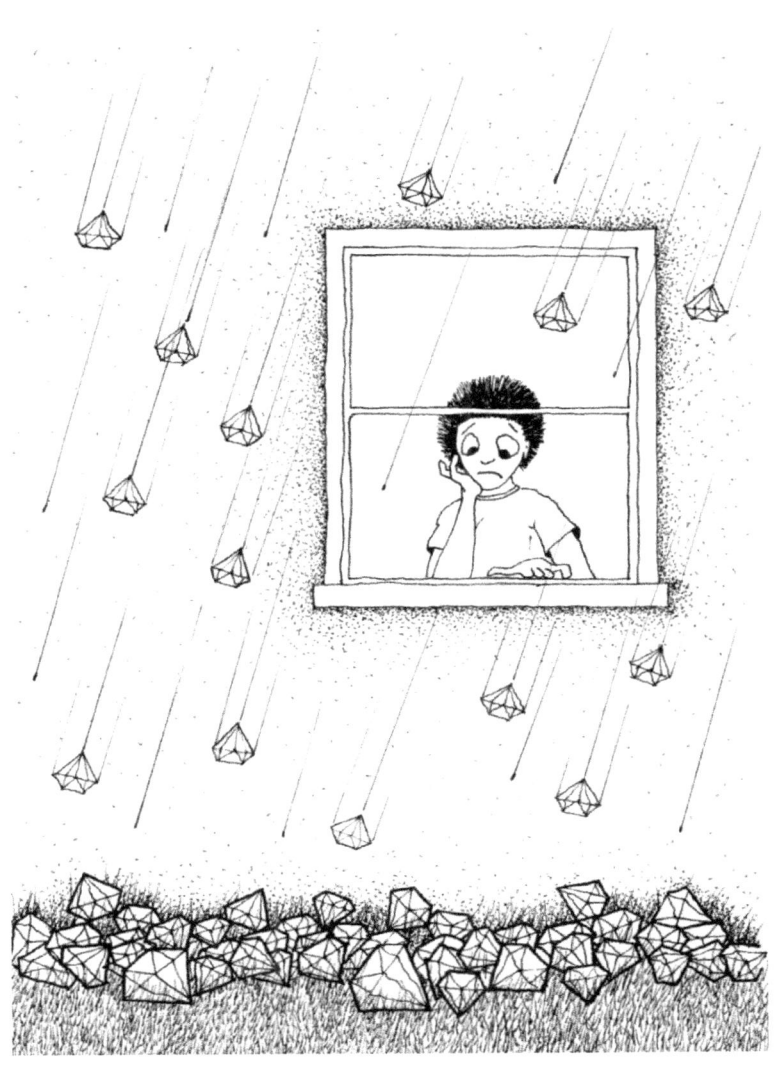

I hate it when I do that and it does this!

The Fly

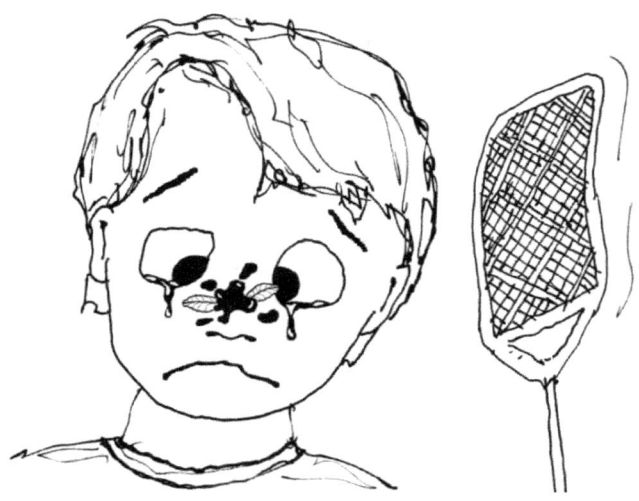

A fly land on my nose,
    And it started to chew.
My Sis said, "I'll help you.
    I know exactly what to do."
Then, with one swift blow,
    And one gigantic splat.
Her aim was perfect.
    She laid that fly out flat.
Now, I sat there half dazed
    As tears in my eyes rose.
With a cringe on my face,
    And fly goo on my nose.
"Sis, thank you for helping.
    You meant well, no doubt.
But next time this happens.
    Please, **don't help me out.**"

Yuck-o Muck-o!
Not this again!

Just day-dreaming away the day...

Lying Up And Looking Down

I was lying on the Earth one day,
My head upon the ground.
I wasn't looking up anymore,
I imagined I was looking down.

Then all of a sudden around me,
Things were different to my eyes.
The trees that once grew straight up,
Now pointed straight down…
…towards the sky.

Clouds that floated over the Earth
Were now drifting slowly under,
And birds were flying beneath the trees,
And built their nests there under.

Cars and buses and people
Were now hanging off the ground,
And everything that was standing up
Was now hanging upside down.

So, once I get to my feet again,
And take a look around,
I won't be standing up anymore,
I'll be **standing down.**

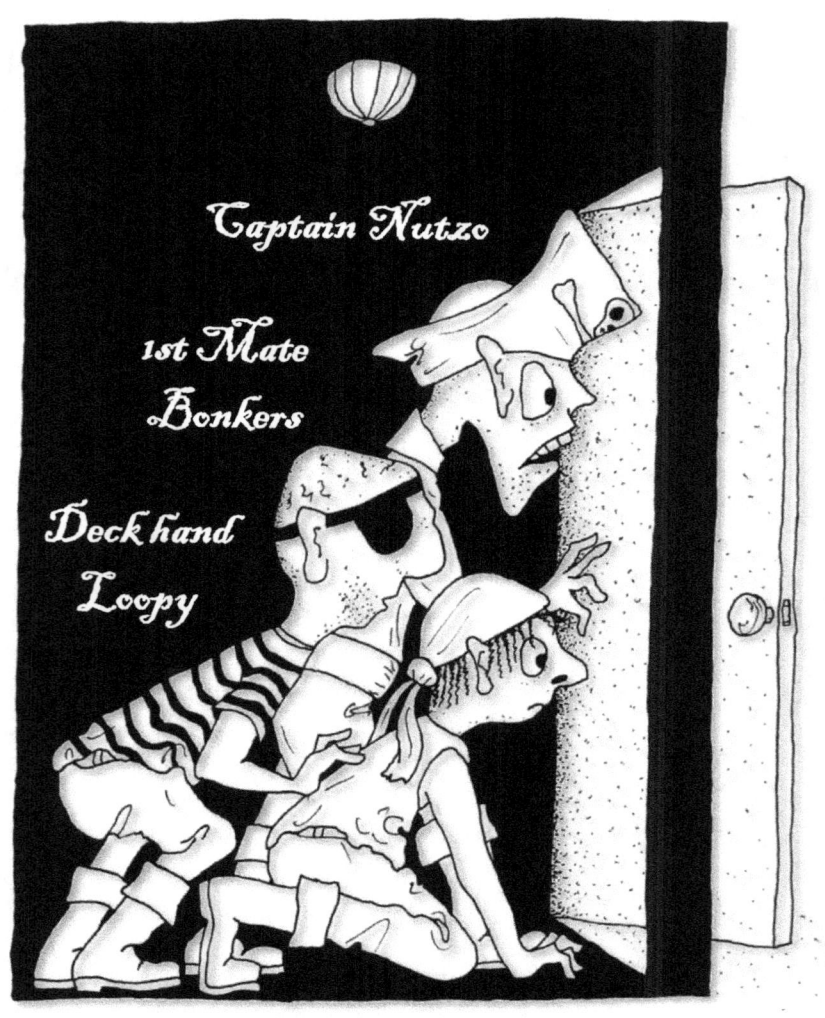

Closet Pirates

There are just some times
When sleepless nights are made.
From the Pirates in my closet
That are keeping me awake.
>They fidget and they fumble.
>They grumble, gripe and groan.
>They sneak into my room at night
>When I am all alone.

They try on all my clothes.
They scatter my toys about.
They're rude and they're obnoxious.
They toot and spit and shout.
>Good manners, they don't have.
>They pick their nose and ears.
>They run into my closet
>When anyone else gets near.

But in spite of all their naughtiness
They're fun to have around.
They always make me laugh,
And pick me up when I'm feeling down.
Now, my Mom thinks it's me
That's not putting my things away.
But I don't mind . . .
. . . cleaning up after them,
If my **Closet Pirates can stay.**

Close To Shore

Have you ever been under the ocean
When the ocean's close to shore.
And seen all the sea life.
The seaweed, fish and more?

With colors you can't imagine,
So rich and blue and green.
It's only near the shore
Where these colors can be seen.

The sunlight that shines down,
And the patterns that are made,
Create such a beautiful place
On the **floor beneath the waves.**

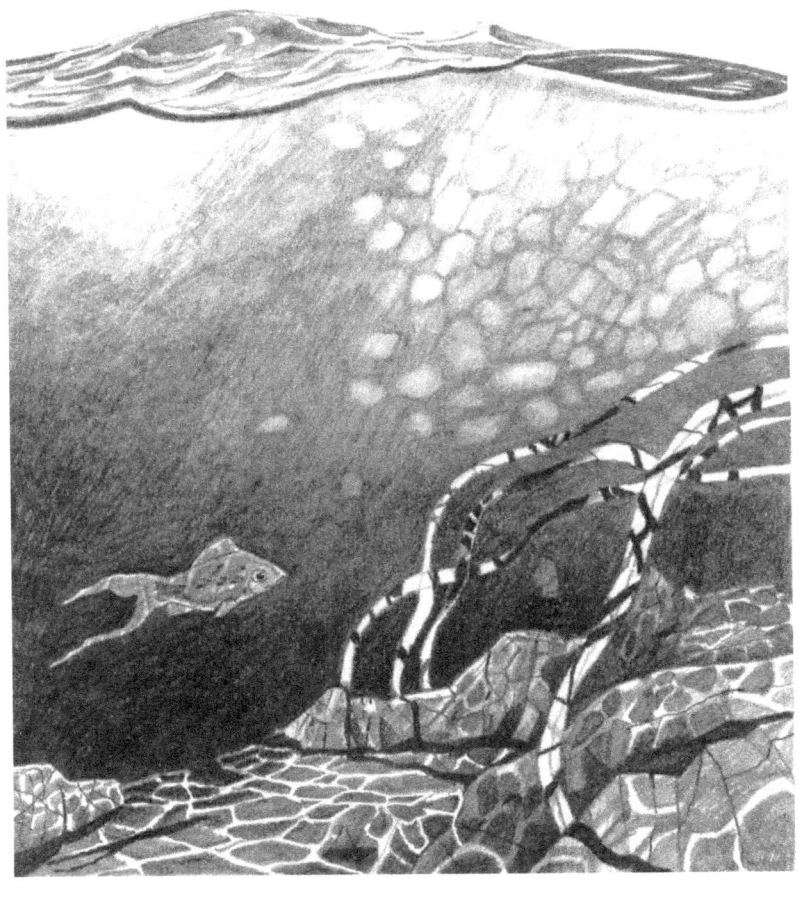

Baseball

When I joined the baseball team
I got a blue jersey and red hat.
I know that I can hit the ball.
If I ever get up to bat.

I want to play on first base,
Or maybe on the mound.
I can just hear them shouting
As the bases I whiz around.

But, I got stuck in center field.
Much to my surprise.
I spend my time looking . . .
. . . at the sky,
And swatting at the flies.

*Hey! Bob,
Bill, Dave,
Sam and Joe. I
thought I told
you guys to stay
at home!*

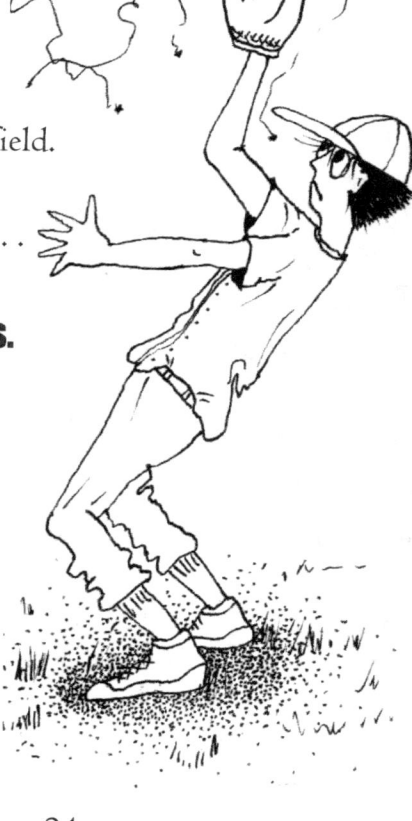

Sun Up

Sun up.
    Wake up.
Open up.
    Look up.
Get up.
    Stand up.
Pull up.
    Dress up.
Pick up.
    Wash up.
Brush up.
    Show up.
Sit up.
    Eat up.
Finish up.
Now!
What's up?

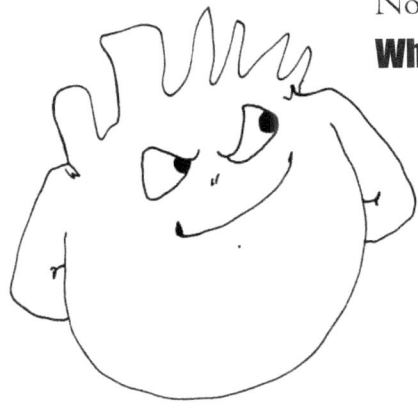

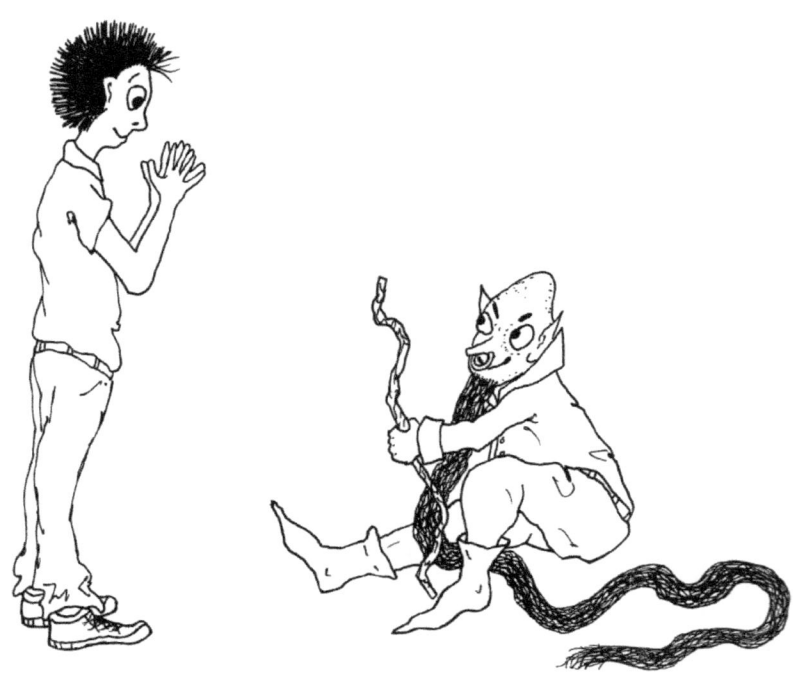

I have an idea!

I'm In Trouble Tomorrow

I'm always getting into trouble.
Even when I'm trying not to.
I wish I could go into the future,
And see what it is I shouldn't do.

Then I heard a voice behind me say,
"I can make your wish come true.
I can send you into the future.
If that's what you'd like to do."

As I turned around I saw
That a strange little Elf had appeared.
He had a ring in his nose and . . .
. . . a stick in his hand,
And a 10 foot long red beard.

"I'm a Red Beard Time Elf," he said,
As he sat down and cocked his head,
"You might not like what you . . .
. . . find in the future.
Maybe you'd better stay here instead."

"Oh! Please send me into . . .
. . . the future," I begged,
"I would really like some help from you.
I want to stop from getting into trouble.
I want to know what I shouldn't do."

"O.K.," he said as he waved his stick.
Then my whole room started to spin.
I was shot into the future just that fast,
And in a flash I was back again.

"What did you find out?" he said,
"Did you get what you wanted to know?"
"Yes." I said, "But, don't send me back.
I'm already in **trouble tomorrow.**"

Have You Ever

Have you ever heard the flutter
Of a thousand butterflies?
Have you ever seen an Aurora
As its colors paint the sky?

Have you ever taken a walk
Guided only by the moonlight?
Have you ever seen an eagle
As it lifts off into flight?

Have you ever tasted water
From a clean forest stream?
Have you ever seen a purple mountain
In the light of fading sun beams?

These few wondrous things
Are the magic of a land.
If you can't do them where you are,
Then go to where you can.

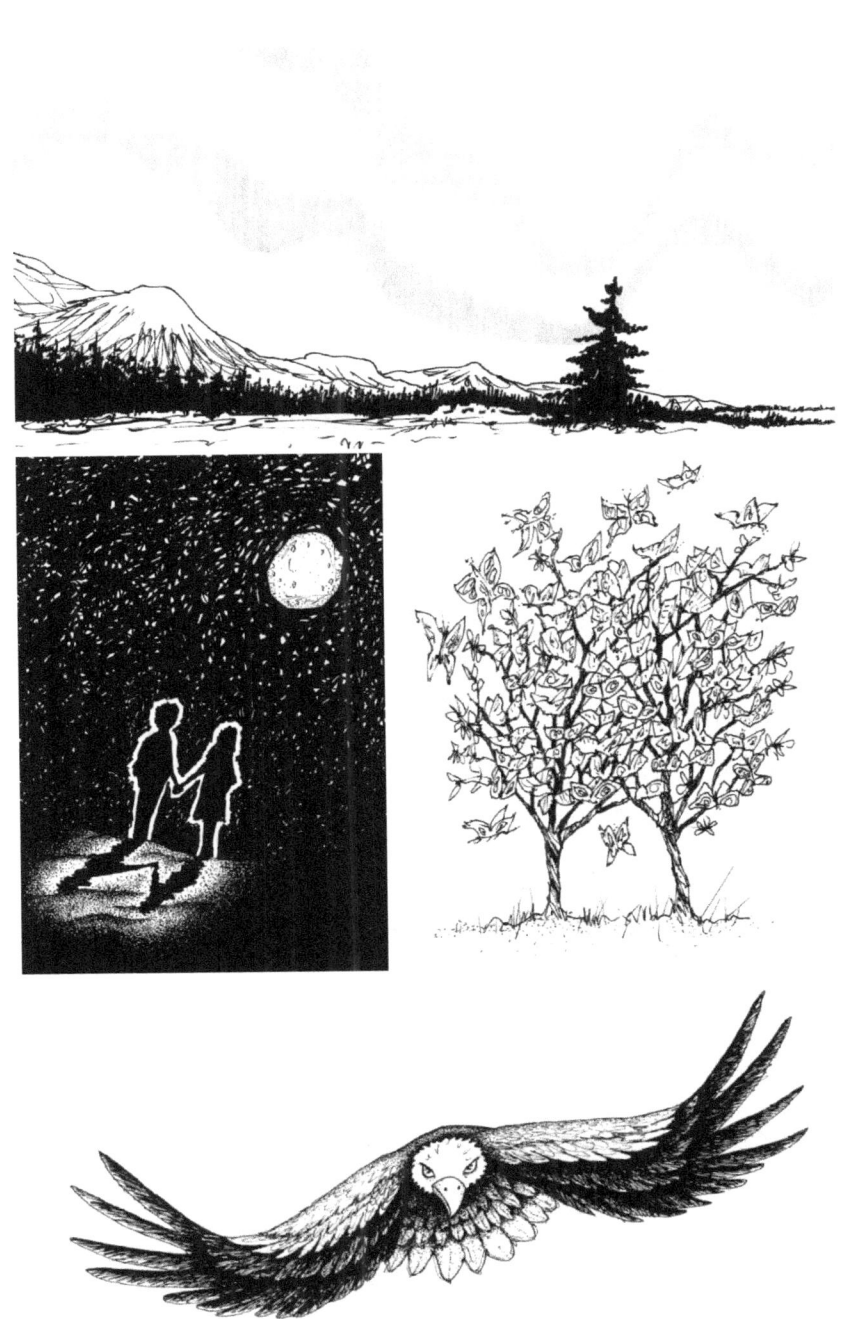

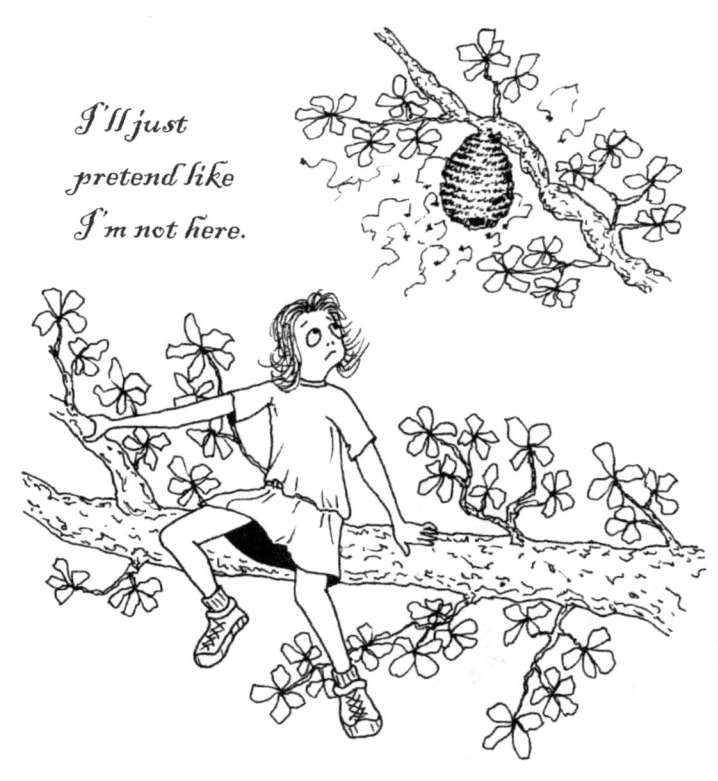

I'll just pretend like I'm not here.

Sitting In A Tree

Just sitting in a tree.
It's wonderful to be,
Up here by myself.
No one to bother me.

I love the peaceful feeling.
The warm and gentle breeze.
The swaying of the branches.
The sound of rustling leaves.

But, I have just one complaint.
One small and tiny need.
It's not very much,
But how do you **get rid of bees?**

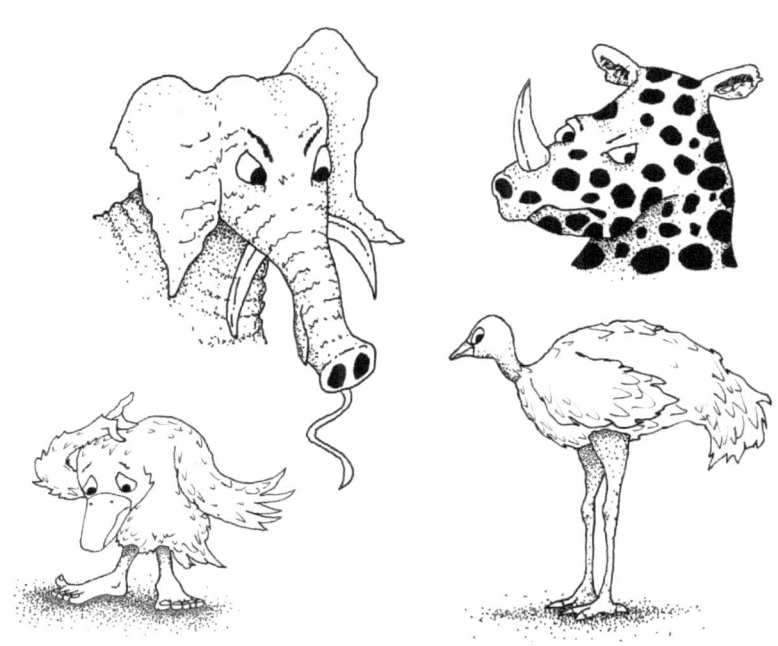

It's Good To Know

Aardvarks have . . .
. . . long tongues.
Leopards wear spots.
Cheetahs are hard to beat,
And dalmatians have dots.

Ducks have web feet.
Crocodiles have bumps.
Ostriches have long necks,
And camels have humps.

Elephants have trunks.
Kangaroos have pouches.
Porcupines have quills,
And sleeping bears are…
…grouches.

Rhinos have horns,
And robins are red breasted.
It's good to know these…
…things
Just in case I get tested.

"Gosh! I hope I don't get them mixed up?"

QUESTIONS

4. IN BETWEEN
   A. Where was Billy clean? *In between his toes*
   B. What was rising behind Billy? *A cloud of dust*
   C. What covered the floor? *Muck*
6. DID THE SUN COME UP
   A. Where was the boy? *In bed*
   B. What did he not want do? *Get up*
7. THE GRUMPY OLD MAN
   A. Where was the old man? *In a grumpy old chair on a grumpy old porch*
   B. What did the old man need to change? *His grumpy old underwear*
8. DRAGONS UNDERNEATH
   A. What happened to the asphalt? *It cracked*
   B. What things were bumping around? *Dragons*
10. I CAN'T GO OUT
    A. What did the boy have? *The chicken pox*
    B. What did he do? *Played connect the dots*
11. BEING GOOD IS HARD
    A. Who did he have to be nice to? *His brother and sister*
    B. When did he try to be nice? *Yesterday*
12. MY PET MONSTER FRED
    A. What is Fred made of? *Spare monster parts*
    B. Where did she find Fred? *At a garage sale*
    C. What did she feed Fred? *Monster soup*
    D. Where does Fred stay? *In a nest at the foot of the bed*
    C. What does Fred do? *Scares all the other monsters away*
14. THE MOUNTAIN STREAM
    A. Where does the stream run through? *The trees*
    B. What should you do there? *Not litter and clean up after yourself*
16. IT'S RAINING DSIAMONDS
    A. Why can't he go outside? *He got in trouble*
    B. What does he want the weather to do? *Rain diamonds again tomorrow*
18. THE FLY
    A. What was on his nose? *Fly goo*
    B. What did his sister do? *Laid the fly out flat with one giant splat*
19. LYING UP AND LOOKING DOWN
    A. Where was his head? *On the ground*
    B. Where were the cars, busses and people? *Hanging off the ground*
    C. Where were the birds? *Flying beneath the trees*
21. CLOSET PIRATES
    A. How many pirates are there? *3*
    B. What did they do to his cloths? *They tried them all on*
22. CLOSE TO SHORE
    A. What colors can be seen? *Blues and greens*
    B. Where are patterns made? *On the sea floor beneath the waves*
24. BASEBALL
    A. What color was his hat? *Red*
    B. What color was his jersey? *Blue*
    C. What was he swatting? *Flies*
    D. What was he looking at? *The sky*
25. SUN UP
    A. What happened after sun up? *Wake up*
26. I'M IN TROUBLE TOMORROW
    A. What kind of Elf was it? *A Red Beard Time Elf*
    B. What happened to his room? *It started to spin*
    C. What did he find out? *That he was in trouble tomorrow*
28. HAVE YOU EVER
    A. How many butterflies? *1,000*
    B. What colors the sky? *An aurora*
30. SITTING IN A TREE
    A. What was her complaint? *Getting rid of the bees*
31. IT'S GOOD TO KNOW
    A. What are sleeping bears? *Grouches*
    B. Why is it good to know these things? *In case he gets tested*
    C. What do Leopards wear? *Spots*

www.ingramcontent.com/pod-product-compliance
Lightning Source LLC
Chambersburg PA
CBHW070846220526
45466CB00002B/895